Rhodesian Despatches

QUARTERLY COLLECTION
VOLUME I

Rhodesian

Despatches

Issue No. 1, January 2021

CONTENTS

Introduction

Welcome to the first quarterly edition of 'Rhodesian Despatches', a publication comprising three individual and consecutive monthly or bi-monthly issues. There will be many more to follow.

I have voluntarily undertaken to produce this publication as part of my overall contribution to the preservation of Rhodesia's military history, covering the whole period of its existence from 1890 until the country became known as Zimbabwe in 1980.

This includes

- the formative 1890s, including the settlement by white pioneers and the indigenous rebellions against their presence;
- the Second Boer War of 1899 to 1902, which saw Rhodesia's oldest territorial force, the Rhodesia Regiment being raised, primarily to defend Rhodesia's borders from Boer aggression;
- World War One that saw white and black Rhodesian soldiers and policemen on active service in East Africa, German South West Africa and Western Europe;
- World War Two, with various elements of the Rhodesian army and air force deployed in East Africa, the Rhodesian African Rifles in Southeast Asia, and hundreds of Rhodesians volunteering for service in the Royal Air Force, Royal Navy, and various arms of the British Army and South African forces, in particular the 6th (South African) Armoured Division in Italy;
- The Malayan Emergency of the 1950s in which the forerunner of C Squadron (Rhodesia) Special Air Service participated, together with the Rhodesian African Rifles;
- Rhodesia's counter-insurgency war of 1966 to 1979.
- In turn, each issue has sections covering a 'Sitrep' (army talk for situation report), 'They Served' (prominent individuals or units), 'Combat', 'Above and Beyond' (honours and awards for bravery and conspicuous service) and 'Field of Grounded Arms' (honouring those who died in conflict serving Rhodesia).

As a non-fiction published author and professional researcher of military history, I naturally go to great lengths to ensure the veracity of my work. I firmly believe in the inclusion of images, maps and diagrams for the benefit of the reader. Wherever possible, I do acknowledge my sources, but following all the political and social changes in Zimbabwe since 1980, this can sometimes be difficult. I therefore apologise if some material appears to lack the appropriate credits. If the reader finds any that may have slipped through, please let me know.

This, the first of such publications, is as a direct response to the many calling for me to publish the Rhodesian Despatches which, since 2021, I have compiled for the global Rhodesian Services Association.

More recently, I was approached by Dr Anne Samson, among others a military historian, researcher and publisher, with an offer to publish my work through her publishing house, TSL Publications UK. Anne shares my great passion for the subject, specialising in East African conflicts. My sincere thanks to all the hard work she injects into our joint ventures.

Above all, enjoy reading 'Rhodesian Dispatches' — I hope you will find it informative and interesting. I do not participate in controversial or political matters, so the onus is on the reader to draw their own conclusions where necessary from the facts presented in my work.

Gerry van Tonder
Derby, England
2025

Colonel John Anthony 'Jack' Spreckley CMG

As the South African War of 1899-1902 gained momentum, Colonel Spreckley of E Squadron, Rhodesia regiment, joined Major General Herbert Plumer's force in the relief of Mafeking. Later, while on patrol on 20 August 1900, his party was surrounded by a group of Transvaalers who, being dressed in khaki, were first taken for friends. When the mistake was discovered, and Lieutenant Spreckley and his party were called upon to surrender, he reputedly replied, "Never give in to them, lads," and was immediately shot dead.

By his death, Rhodesia lost one of its best known and most popular men. He saw much service during that war and the early days of Matabeleland. On 7 May 1897, Spreckley had been appointed a Companion of the Order of St Michael and St George for his services in the Matabele Rebellion.

Spreckley was born in 1865 at Fulbeck, near Lincoln, in England, and left for South Africa in 1881, where he worked for four years on an ostrich farm in Grahamstown, before the lure of gold took him to the Witwatersrand. In 1885, he joined the Bechuanaland Border Police (BBP), but, after only a year, joined his companions Frank Johnson, Maurice Heany, Henry Borrow and Ted Burnett to seek a concession from Lobengula to prospect for gold in that part of the world. The amaNdebele king begrudgingly granted them permission, but the party found little of value in the streams and rivers along the Mazoe River. Upon arriving back in GuBulawayo, the young adventurers were forced to pay a fine of £100 in gold sovereigns to Lobengula, for alleged misconduct in the interior.

Spreckley (above), however, remained unsettled, briefly staying in Kimberley before moving to Johannesburg for a couple of years. A bad case of fever saw him on the move again, this time down to Durban, and then by sea to Cape Town, where he wanted to recuperate in the milder climate. Here he again met up with his prospecting companions and, upon hearing that an expedition was being planned into Mashonaland, he joined the Pioneer Corps as Paymaster-Sergeant.

Signing up on 30 May 1890, Spreckley reunited with his earlier friends, now all serving as commissioned officers under the leadership of Major Frank Johnson. With the column in training at Camp Cecil on the banks of the Limpopo River in Bechuanaland, Spreckley was assigned to A Troop under the command of Maurice Heany, before later being transferred to B Troop, where he was appointed Market Master to the column.

After the founding of Fort Salisbury and the disbandment of the column, Spreckley, together with so many of his companions, struck out into the veld in search of 'El Dorado'. By June 1892, he had become the Mining Commissioner for the Lomagundi District, basing himself at a site where the settlement of Sinoia developed.

Towards the end of that year, Spreckley travelled back to Britain with Henry Borrow, where he met his future wife in the form of Borrow's sister, Beatrice. He returned to Salisbury in June 1893, to be given command of C Troop of the Salisbury Horse which, together with A Troop under Heany and B Troop under Borrow, would form part of the Salisbury Column under the command of Major Patrick Forbes that would march on to GuBulawayo to subdue the amaNdebele.

Joining up with Major Allan Wilson's Victoria Column at Iron Mine Hill on 2 October, the first engagement with Lobengula's impis took place on the Shangani River on 25 October, followed a few days later by the Battle of Bembesi. On 4 November, the force entered a deserted, burning GuBulawayo, the king having fled north in his wagon. A pursuit column was organised under Forbes' command, which included 90 men of the Salisbury Column, with officers Spreckley and Heany. The rest of the task force was made up of just over 200 men of the Victoria Column.

As the column progressed, rations started running low and dissatisfaction among many of the troops grew, culminating in Forbes holding a meeting with some of the men and subsequently sending back all the Salisbury men including Spreckley, except for 22 under Borrow, a fateful decision as it turned out for Spreckley's dear friend. Spreckley and Johnson would erect a pulpit memorial in the Anglican Cathedral, Salisbury, carrying the inscription, 'To the Glory of God and in memory of Henry John Borrow. Killed at Shangani December 4th, 1893'.

Spreckley led 67 men of the Salisbury Horse back to Fort Salisbury, their numbers significantly reduced through the war, and many others electing to stay in Matabeleland.

Bulawayo laager defences, Matabele Rebellion, 1896

Spreckley was later appointed magistrate of Fort Victoria, and ten months thereafter returned to Bulawayo where he became General Manager of Sir John Willoughby's gold mining company. It was here, on 31 August 1895, that Spreckley married Beatrice Borrow and decided to settle down. Political events in the sub-continent, however, would come close to embroiling Spreckley in the debacle that was the Jameson Raid. Willoughby joined the raiding party, handing over command of the Rhodesia Horse to Spreckley, together with various letters which were only to be opened if 'certain' events were to take place. Spreckley would receive telegraphed instructions that the Rhodesia Horse must not under any circumstances move to assist Jameson. This telegraph and other letters left in Spreckley's care almost implicated him in Jameson's impetuous adventure.

At the outbreak of the Matabele Rebellion, Frederick Courteney Selous, fearing for the safety of his wife at their farm in Essexvale, placed her in the care of the Spreckleys. Spreckley himself was now appointed a colonel in the Bulawayo Field Force and second-in-command to Colonel William Napier.

Spreckley and Bulawayo's Mayor Scott had been very instrumental in laagering Bulawayo and establishing 'order out of chaos'. During the insurrection, Spreckley saw action at Umguza River where his force, together with elements of the Afrikander Corps and the Grey's Scouts, engaged and routed a 1,000-strong impi of amaNdebele, and led numerous patrols.

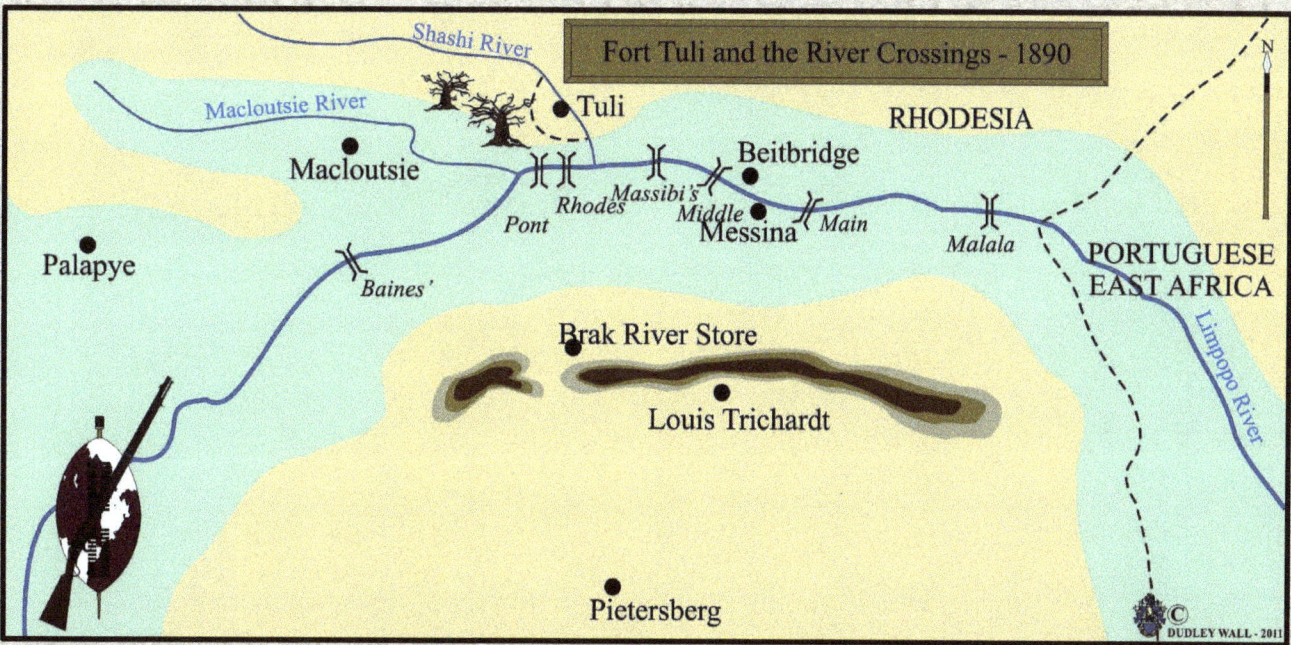

Fort Tuli and the River Crossings - 1890

Shashi River · Tuli · RHODESIA · Macloutsie River · Macloutsie · Beitbridge · Massibi's · Rhodes Pont · Middle · Messina · Main · Malala · Palapye · Baines' · PORTUGUESE EAST AFRICA · Limpopo River · Brak River Store · Louis Trichardt · Pietersberg · N · © DUDLEY WALL - 2011

In the early stages of the Anglo-Boer War, Colonel Spreckley, now officer commanding A Squadron, was part of Colonel Herbert Plumer's force based at Fort Tuli. Plumer's task was to defend the various drifts across the Limpopo, Macloutsie and Shashi rivers from being used by Boer forces to infiltrate Rhodesia.

On 2 November 1899, 400 men from the Zoutpansberg Commando circled around Spreckley's position at Rhodes Drift and headed into Rhodesia. The Transvaalers struck at Bryce's Store, overwhelming a convoy of wagons carrying supplies to Spreckley. Fearing for the safety of Fort Tuli, Plumer recalled all his squadrons, but Spreckley found himself in a very difficult situation, as the enemy started shelling his position, killing nearly all the animals.

His retreat was cut off and his defences exposed in the rear. Typical of so much of the questionable tactics that would characterise the strategies of the Boers during the war, the commando did not close in on Spreckley, preferring to pin him down with fire from their Mauser rifles. Spreckley and his men lay motionless until nightfall, when they silently crept away in the dark, around the enemy position and north back to Tuli.

The next morning the Boers again shelled the position now vacated by Spreckley and his squadron, but it was only at noon that they discovered that their adversary had gone. In another surprising decision, the commando entrenched themselves at the store instead of carrying out an assault on a very vulnerable Fort Tuli.

The official British history of the South African War records the pursuit by British forces of 246 Free Staters under the elusive General de Wet, east through the Magaliesberg Mountains away from the recent battle at Elands River. Various other Boer commandos were also present in the area north of Pretoria, trying to consolidate their forces with de Wet. Baden-Powell and Colonel T.E. Hickman, with some 800 mounted men and half a battalion of the West Riding Regiment in ox-wagons, moved north of Hammanskraal on 19 August 1900, in pursuit of a Boer commando. Included in this force were 'A' and 'E' Squadrons of the Rhodesia Regiment under Lt Colonel Spreckley.

As Major-General Arthur Paget's forces struck out on the northern road close to the railway line, Baden-Powell moved forward on the right across the Pienaar's River, with the Rhodesia Regiment covering his advance. Spreckley suddenly came upon a party of 100 mounted Boers of the Waterberg Commando, precipitating a fight which left Colonel Spreckley and four of his men dead: Sergeant George Blurt on, corporals Robert Caffyn, and Alexander Downis, all of A Squadron, and Trooper Francis Forster of E Squadron.

Colonel Spreckley was originally buried in the Hammanskraal Cemetery, near where he died. Many years later, his remains, together with those of other British soldiers buried in the area, were dug up and interred in a military cemetery at Petronella.

Rhodesian African Rifles, Malayan Emergency

On 9 November 1956, information was received of a British patrol in the Bahau area of Malaya having a fleeting engagement with Chinese communist terrorists (CTs) under Hor Lung, which was heading towards the Palong River. A and B companies, 1st Battalion, Rhodesian African Rifles, were immediately moved from the Bekok area to take up positions alongside C and D companies, where the Muar River was so swollen from persistent heavy rain, that collapsible boats had to be employed to effect a crossing.

A half-section from Second Lieutenant de Bruyn's 7 Platoon saw 16 pack-laden CTs moving east. Section Commander Corporal Munyameni, not holding out for commands, launched an immediate attack. Caught unawares, the CTs bombshelled in all directions. One CT, trying to appear invisible behind the bole of a tree was shot and killed.

Early that same morning, C Company's 8 Platoon, commanded by the newly promoted—and acting company commander—Lieutenant 'Digger' Essex-Clark, was patrolling back towards company HQ. He had split his platoon into three-man sections to cover more ground. A platoon corporal led his half-section to the west, while Essex-Clark with a rifleman and the Bren gunner headed southeast.

The officer led his two men across a deep swampy creek, or sungai, before coming to a halt, straining their ears for any indication of human presence. Essex-Clark continues:

Digger Essex-Clark with soldiers from 8 Platoon, Rhodesian African Rifles, Malaya 1957. (Digger Essex-Clark)

> A weird feeling often alerts me to a threat before sight or sound reaches me. I spin around to the east, diving to the ground, Patchett ready, before the crackling 9mm fire and the rhythmic 'thump-thump-thump thump-thump, of a Bren echoes through the jungle, blending with the crump of shot guns and faint shouts. I had just been thinking that Hor Lung had got away so I hope our patrols have not run into one another. Then with the distinctive 'crang' of grenades, which we do not carry, I know that we have a contact with terrorists. We melt into a three-man ambush on the ridge and wait.

Forty metres away, in a densely foliaged creek, we hear a group bashing its way downstream. We catch glimpses of their khaki uniforms: CTs! They are moving fast towards the Palong and are now past our patrols. I crab-scuttle down the flat ridge behind us and hear Mabgwe and Zacha [his men] following me. We'll cut them off and attempt to engage them closer at the point where the creek wends its way close to the northern spur of our ridge.

We reach the swampy creek at the same time as the CTs are scurrying by. They're on the far bank and not easy to see clearly but there seem to be about six of them armed with rifles and Sten guns. They're chirruping and urging each other on in Chinese. Fair odds. We three have the initiative. They have not shot at us; therefore they have not seen us. We run, crouched, and crawl closer to find better firing positions. They see us first and fire wildly. We fire back and charge in. I shoot at two CTs 25 metres in front of me. One is firing at me; he stumbles; I fire and bowl him over, but I can't see my lads with me.

Bullets thump into trees near me. I feel alone but keep scrambling forward. I fire my 'signature', a one three double tap, twice, to let the others know where I am. Thunk. My Patchett jams! I mutter. I change magazines. Still jammed. I can hear firing on my left: Mabgwe. 'Get up with me you dingwit!' I mutter. I look in the ejection opening. It is plugged with moss and crud. I drop into the lopak [Malay: pool or puddle] swamp behind a log and quickly clear out the mess with my finger. It burns. I see blood mixed in the water. Not mine. I've lost my jungle hat and feel awkward and exposed without it. I bind my head with my sweat rag and roll forward over the log. A spray of bullets showers me with muck. They must know that there are only three of us.

Rhodesian African Rifles jungle ambush, Malaya. (RAR Regt Assoc, UK)

I scramble sideways and crawl through the swamp, noticing, of all things, dozens of pitcher plants which trap insects. I stand in a tree buttress and fire a burst in the direction of the CTs. I hear Zachariah shout and the thump-thump, thump-thump double-tap of his Bren on my right.

We keep stumbling and scrambling up the incline getting even further behind them. We cannot keep up and we are the ones firing wildly now. They fire back at us with controlled bursts. I can't see them but there now seem to be many more than six. Their bullets cracked overhead. I see blood splattered on a log. 'Steady, buster,' I caution myself. 'You're supposed to be commanding a company, not two men.'

I shout, 'Stop!' The CTs have gone over the ridge line ahead. I give them a short final burst for luck and bravado and put on my last full magazine.

Zachariah joins me. We are both excited, grinning and panting. He has only one magazine left. We find Mabgwe. He's a little shaky and has a badly sprained ankle. Supporting him, we move warily back to the patrol base.

Everyone in the base is euphoric. Our patrols return. We send out search parties for the wounded and the dead. I radio back to headquarters to tell them that we've had a successful contact and will confirm later the details of CTs killed or suspected wounded. I also asked for tracker-dog teams to help us follow-up. It is the battalion's first success, for which we'd trained and waited nearly two years.

I cool down and squat, exhausted, against a tree buttress, next to my radio operator. The body of the dead CT lies next to me on a makeshift stretcher of cut saplings, poncho and nylon cord.

Rhodesian African Rifles Malayan Emergency veteran,
the late Platoon Warrant Officer Pisayi Muzerecho MM,
at the unveiling of the RAR Memorial
in England on 19 July 2015.

Trooper Herbert Stephen Henderson VC

'THE Queen has been graciously pleased to signify Her intention to confer the decoration of the Victoria Cross on the undermentioned Soldier':

Trooper Herbert Stephen Henderson, Bulawayo Field Force, citation:

On the morning of the 30th March, 1896, just before daylight, Captain. Macfarlane's party was surprised by the natives. Troopers Celliers and Henderson, who formed part of the advanced guard, were cut off from the main body, and Celliers was shot through the knee. His horse also was badly wounded and eventually died. Henderson then placed Celliers on his own horse, and made the best of his way to Buluwayo. The country between Campbell's Store, where they were cut off, and Buluwayo, a distance of about thirty-five miles, was full of natives fully armed, and they had, therefore, to proceed principally by night, hiding in the bush in the daytime. Celliers, who was weak from loss of blood, and in great agony, asked Henderson to leave him, but he would not, and brought him in, after passing two days and one night in the veldt without food.
(*The London Gazette*, 7 May 1897)

Rhodesian Corps of Engineers, 5 January 1979

On 5 January 1979, a massive explosion at the Victoria Falls rifle range killed seven members of the Rhodesian Corps of Engineers (RhE).

As a result of sappers being critically injured in the southeast over the previous two days when handling Rhodesian-made Carrot anti-personnel mines, an order was sent out to backload all these mines to the rear HQ for forwarding to Army Ordnance for vetting.

An underground magazine at the Victoria Falls rifle range held stocks of these mines, which were used in the minefields stretching from Victoria Falls to Deka, so a truck driven by Sergeant Adams was sent to this locality to upload the faulty AP mines.

The majority of the engineers based at the Falls were sent there to assist, including the outgoing officer commanding, Lieutenant John Carlisle. Some formed a chain to load the boxes of mines, while others were employed a distance away to recover empty plough-shear boxes. At this time there was an enormous explosion.

The findings of a board of inquiry were inconclusive, estimating that four to five boxes of these mines had detonated. The cost was great—seven men of this unit all lost their lives in this tragedy. (Source: Lieutenant B. Calder who was present at the time.)

650600 Sapper BINGA, Bernard, 1 Squadron RhE
661319 Sapper DUBE, Methuseli, 1 Squadron RhE
650230 Lance Corporal GONYE, Gift, 1 Squadron RhE
644180 Staff Sergeant GWENJERI, Tobias, 1 Squadron RhE
650182 Sapper MAJUTA, Benson, 1 Squadron RhE
99260 Sergeant MORIARTY, Leonard, 1 Squadron RhE
650186 Sapper NYATHI, Lunis, School of Infantry

(Image Dudley Wall)

Rhodesian

Despatches

Issue No. 2, February 2021

CONTENTS

Thanks for all the positive feedback to my first issue of Rhodesian Dispatches last month. In one of these, Don Scott says, "I did not realise the RAR were involved in the Malaya Emergency. Also I don't recall any news announcements at the time of the 7 sappers killed at the Victoria Falls explosion. A news blackout I suppose. I was a member of 2 Engineers at the time."

The 1RAR's tour of duty in Malaya was from 1956 to 1958. Of interest, in March 1951, a 24-year-old Temporary Captain Peter Walls (future commander of the Rhodesian Army) led 100 men of the so-called South East Asia Volunteer Unit (SEAVU) on active service in Malaya. Among their number was Sergeant Ron Reid-Daly, who went on to command the Selous Scouts. The SEAVU was the foundation of the Rhodesian C Squadron, SAS.

Whether by 'accident' or in action, there are other cases of large numbers of Rhodesian troops losing their lives in a single incident, for example, the Puma helicopter shot down in Mozambique in September 1979, killing 14 Rhodesian troops and the SAAF crew of 3, and the 12 members of the RAR who drowned when their vehicle fell into a dam in May 1972. Most of the victims were from the famous RAR band, who were also required to fight in the bush war.

On occasion, press releases were staggered over several days to mask the large number.

The RAR band and troops participated in the Malaya Federation independence celebrations in 1957. Bandmaster Tam Lewis readies the band. (Photo RAR Regt Assoc UK)

Much-respected combatants of the RAR, 1970s.

REMEMBERING PUMA 164
OPERATION URIC
6 SEPTEMBER 1979

S.A.A.F

Pilot:
Capt. Paul Denzel Velleman

Co-Pilot:
Lt. Nigel David Osborne

Flight Engineer:
Sgt. Dirk Wilhelmus Marthinus
(Dick) Retief

Rhodesian Engineers:

Capt. Charles David Small
2nd Lt. Bruce Fraser Burns
Sgt. Michael Alan Jones
Cpl. Leroy Duberley
L/Cpl. Peter Fox

1 Commando
Rhodesian Light Infantry

Capt. Johannes Matheus Duplooy
Cpl. Gordon Hugh Fry
Tpr. Jacobus Alwyn (Koise) Briel
Tpr. Aiden James Coleman
Tpr. Mark Jeremy Crow
Tpr. Brian Louis Enslin
Tpr. Steven Eric King
Tpr. Colin Graham Neassham
Tpr. David Rex Prosser

© Gerry van Tonder

Puma 164 remembered in the Rhodesian Museum in Bedford, England.
(Photo Gerry van Tonder)

Colonel John Banks Brady DSO, OBE, ED

John Banks Brady was born in Ireland in November 1875, and was educated at Middleton College and Trinity College, Dublin. The outbreak of the Anglo-Boer War, he volunteered for the elite 45th 'Irish Hunt' Company, 13th Battalion, Imperial Yeomanry. He was subsequently commissioned into the Commander-in-Chief's Bodyguard, and served in Kitchener's Fighting Scouts.

Remaining in South Africa at the end of the Anglo-Boer War, Brady made rapid progress in his chosen profession in education, becoming Headmaster of Grey College, Bloemfontein, in the Orange River Colony and, in 1909, Chief Inspector of Schools in Southern Rhodesia. He also found time to establish himself as an enthusiastic member of the Rhodesian Volunteers, and on learning of the outbreak of hostilities in August 1914, he immediately sailed for the U.K.

Rapidly commissioned as a lieutenant on the Special List, he was then promoted to captain in the 6th Battalion, King's Royal Rifle Corps (KRRC), where he was given command of No. 16 Platoon, D Company, the 3rd Battalion—called the 'Rhodesian Platoon'—landing with it in France in December 1914. The following year, he was mentioned in dispatches. Transferred to the 2nd Battalion, he was gassed that September at Loos, before being attached to brigade headquarters. He was again mentioned in despatches and awarded the French Croix de Guerre in December 1916.

In 1917, he returned to frontline service, when, in June, he was appointed a Companion of the Distinguished Service Order (DSO), and was mentioned in despatches for a third time.

Brady was subsequently appointed the 1st Battalion's second-in-command, and in January 1918 he assumed overall command with the rank of Temporary Major. He was wounded in action near Le Sars on the Somme, and medically evacuated to Britain.

Having recovered, in July 1918 Brady returned to France, where he rejoined the 1st Battalion prior to becoming commander of the 4th Battalion as a Temporary Lieutenant Colonel towards the end of the year.

During this period he regularly led reconnaissance missions to ensure the best possible outcome for planned attacks, including along the Escaut, between Marquincourt Farm and Quincamp Mill, and again at the crossing of the Selle River. He was again mentioned in dispatches.

On resigning in March 1920, with the rank of honorary Lieutenant Colonel, Brady returned to Southern Rhodesia to continue with his career in education, firstly as Senior Inspector of Schools, and then as Headmaster of Milton School in Bulawayo.

Maintaining his links with the military establishment, he commanded the Bulawayo Military District when the defence system was re-organised, and sat on the Southern Rhodesia Council for Defence. In addition, he was largely responsible for fostering the alliance between the KRRC and Royal Rhodesia Regiment.

In 1930, Brady retired from education and entered politics, being elected an MP for Bulawayo East, a seat which he held until 1946, but it was for the motion he put before the House on 24 August 1939, that he will best be remembered:

"That the Acting Prime Minister request H.E. the Governor to convey to H.M. The King the heartfelt expression of the Honourable Members of this House their humble duty and service to his Throne and person and the pledge of unfaltering service of the citizens of Southern Rhodesia to the Motherland in this hour of grave national emergency".

The motion was carried unopposed, and Brady immediately returned to uniform as a military observer and Southern Rhodesia Liaison Officer to Middle East Command. One of his first tasks was to tour the west coast of Africa, where many Rhodesians were at that time serving in readiness for deployment in the East Africa campaign. he did good service up until being compelled to return to Rhodesia as a result of ill-health.

In June 1943, Brady was appointed an Officer of the Order of the British Empire (OBE).

L-R: Distinguished Service Order (DSO), Officer of the Order of the British Empire (OBE), Queen's South Africa Medal, with clasps 'Cape Colony', 'Orange Free State', 'Transvaal', 'South Africa 1901', 1914-15 Star British War Medal, Victory Medal, with Oak Leaf MID, 1939-45 Star, Africa Star, 1939-45 War Medal, Territorial Decoration, with clasp 'Southern Rhodesia', Croix de Guerre (France) 1914-1918.

Colonel Brady died in Bulawayo General Hospital at the age of 77 years, his obituarist in the King's Royal Rifle Corps Chronicle, noting that 'In his youth he was a fine athlete, particularly on the track, and to the last retained the long, raking stride of the quarter-miler and half-miler'. Military barracks in Bulawayo, the training venue for national conscripts, was named after Brady.

Shot Down Over North Africa

Early days. Left: Lance-corporal Keith Coster of the Special Service Battalion, 1937. Centre: officer cadet during flying training, 1939. Rudder belongs to a Blenheim. Right Lieutenant, South African Air Force. Coster spent the last three years of the war in POW camps in Italy and Germany (where he roomed with author Paul Brickhill, and took a part in the Great Escape).

(*Illustrated Life* Rhodesia, 27 January 1971)

Keith Coster, future commander of the Rhodesian Army 1968 to 1972, at the age of 17 attested into the Union Defence Force (UDF) on 6 July 1937, joining the Special Service Battalion (SSB), the Royal Durban Light Infantry (RDLI).

Earning his pilot's wings in the South African Air Force in September 1939, after extensive war training and with the rank of captain, Coster was deployed to the Middle East in April 1942, where he was transferred to No. 5 Squadron, No. 7 Wing SAAF, No. 233 Wing (Royal Air Force) RAF, No. 212 Group RAF.

In 2015, I was privileged to receive from General Coster's son, Steve, a large quantity of his late father's personal papers, certificates, photographs and items of uniform. Included were his memoirs of his military career from pilot and POW in World War Two, officer in the Federation of Rhodesia and Nyasaland Army, General Officer Commanding the Rhodesian Army, and finally as a key advisor to South African Prime Minister P.W. Botha when he served on that country's State Security Council.

In his own words, this is the exclusive account of Coster's air combat over the Western Desert of the North African theatre, which resulted in him being shot down and taken prisoner:

> On 2nd July 1942, we were ferried out to LG (Landing Ground) 85 in the desert, to join what was known as 233 Wing, which consisted of No's 2, 4 and 5 Squadrons of the South African Air Force, but which was commanded by a Group Captain Beresford of the Royal Air Force.
>
> I was assigned to No. 5 Squadron, which was equipped with Tomahawks. Dick Clifton, much to my envy, went to No. 4 Squadron, which had Kittyhawks, which were much superior to the 'Tommies'. Fighter squadrons usually had 12 operational aircraft, seldom more, and often less if there had been casualties.

The CO (Commanding Officer) of No. 5 Squadron up to a few days before had been Dennis Lacey. He had been shot down and killed, as had 'Cookie' Botha, one of my fellow cadets who, in the time that we had been at OTU, had shot down five enemy aircraft, been awarded a DFC, and then had been shot down himself. Our Acting CO at that stage was a Captain van der Spuy.

The next day, July 3rd 1942, saw my first operational sortie, which lasted an hour and five minutes. Our task was close-escort to 12 Bostons bombers, which were bombing 10 miles southwest of El Alamein. This was a relatively uneventful sortie as we were not attacked from the air, but had plenty of flak coming up at us. Flak was the air force name for German anti-aircraft shells, timed to burst at the height at which the formation was flying. Although most of the flak was aimed at the bomber formation, a good deal of it also came the way of the fighter escort.

One knew that if one was unfortunate enough to fly into one of these 'black puffs'; it could in the worst instance prove fatal. So to be hit by flak was unlucky. My next op was on 6th July; also a close-escort job for 12 Bostons bombing 5 miles east of El Daba. It was equally uneventful.

The following day, I was part of the first cover for 18 Bostons, again bombing in the Alamein area. First-cover was not as close to the bomber formation as close-escort, but still got its fair share of flak. Most fighter operations lasted about an hour.

A Curtiss P-40 Tomahawk of No. 5 Squadron, SAAF, Libya, 1942.

On 9th July, I flew two sorties, one at 0830 in the morning, which was an offensive sweep to find the Luftwaffe. We did in fact encounter two Messerschmitt Bf 109s, who pushed off when they saw that they were outnumbered.

Our second op that day was at 11:05: another close escort to the bomber formation consisting of thirteen Bostons and five Baltimores. The op on 10 July was to be our last from LG85 and called for No. 5 Squadron to provide medium cover to 18 Bostons bombing south of El Daba. At this stage, I had been involved in close escort, first cover and medium cover duties.

The other form of cover to bombers was known as top cover. Later that day, 10th July, all the 5 Squadron pilots made a 30 minute 'communication' flight from LG85 to LG97 as the land battle shifted slightly in the favour of the German land forces, known as the Afrika Korps, and they advanced closer to Cairo.

All the air force units had to move back closer to Cairo too. Little did I realise when I took off the next day that I would not see LG97 again – ever. I recall that on the night of 10th July there was a German air raid on Alexandria, the Egyptian seaport on the Mediterranean. One of the No. 5 Squadron pilots, Ray Armstrong, and I sat on the edge of a slit-trench dug into the desert sand, and watched the German bombers flying over our heads towards 'Alex', which was not very far away. One could see the Allied searchlights probing the night sky, hear the bombs exploding and the anti-aircraft guns hammering away. Ray Armstrong survived the war but I did not see him again for at least three years.

The next day, 11th July, I was assigned to a medium cover operation to 18 Bostons and we took off in the early afternoon. Flying as my 'number two' was a young 2nd Lieutenant called Lionel Rapp. His function was to keep an eye open for any attacks from enemy fighters and thus to protect my rear. We were flying at about 8000 feet when all of a sudden, we were ordered over the radio to attack a formation of German Stukas that were dive bombing Allied forces in the same general area as our Bostons were going to bomb in. Almost immediately, I spotted them – and they obviously had seen us – because they stopped their dive bombing and headed downwards with their throttles wide open. My No. 5 Squadron formation broke away from the Bostons and dived in pursuit of the Stukas. As we hurtled towards the ground, the first thing of which I became aware was out of the corner of my left eye: a burning Tomahawk completely enveloped in flames. I presumed it was Lionel Rapp, which was later confirmed. It could mean only one thing: our formation had been 'jumped by ME 109s, just as we had jumped the Stukas.

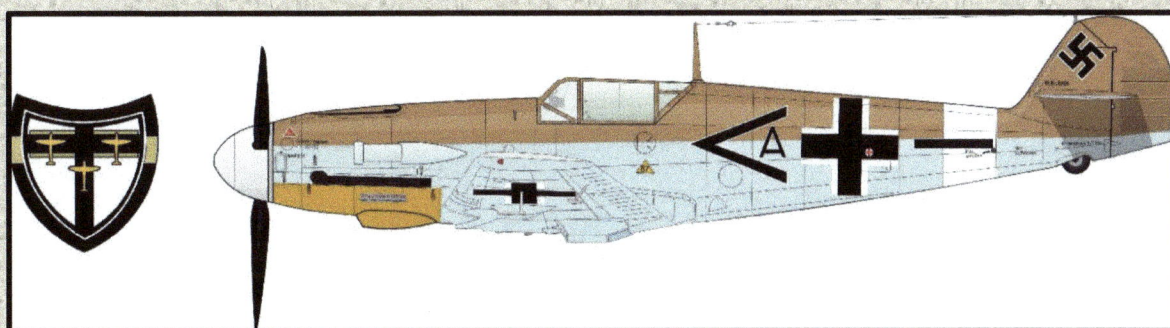

Messerschmitt Bf 109, Jagdgeschwader 47, North Africa 1942. (Drawing Col Dudley Wall)

At this point I had my sights on a Stuka and I fired my four .50 Browning guns at him. I know I damaged the Stuka, but whether he went down or not I don't know, because I became pre-occupied with a sudden loss of my ring-sight that normally imaged on the windscreen in front of my face. We all pulled out of our dive as we were getting dangerously close to the ground, and as I levelled out, there was an almighty bang. I realised that I had been hit!

While I was absorbing this development, a 109 passed in front of me and I gave him a burst from my Brownings – but it was not an aimed burst as my ring sight had gone. In trying to follow the 109, it became immediately obvious that my rudder had been shot away because there was no response when I kicked my rudder bar. An aircraft without a rudder becomes a sitting duck, as the basic manoeuvre in aerial combat is to turn into any aircraft that fires at you.

It was obvious that without rudder control I couldn't make any further contribution to the dogfight, so by the use of ailerons alone, I managed to start a long flat turn towards the sea when I was hit again. Not being able to turn into my attacker, I had but two alternatives: to climb or to dive. I decided on the latter and dived down to a few hundred feet above the ground.

In the dive I was hit a third time from directly behind – a long burst which started my Tomahawk burning and caused shrapnel wounds in my left arm and in my neck. I could see the long trail of smoke tailing out behind my aircraft and I knew that I had to make a very quick decision. To climb to a height where I could bail out would be inviting further – and probably fatal – attacks, or a complete burnout of the aircraft.

As I was very close to the ground, I decided to put it down on the desert and get out before it went up in flames. I loosened my straps and jumped clear before the aircraft had come to a halt. When I stopped rolling, I jumped to my feet and ran to put as much distance as I could between me and the aeroplane. Seconds later, it burst into flames and very rapidly burnt out completely.

I continued running, but could see the Me 109 turning and diving down towards me. Then he opened up, and a couple of cannon shells exploded close enough to me to cause rock fragments to penetrate the skin under my jaw. I fell forward as though I had been fatally wounded, and lay spread-eagled on the desert sand. The Me 109 pilot did another circuit to see whether I would get up again, but as I didn't, he presumably considered me dead and flew home to his forward landing ground. When I was satisfied that there was no more aerial activity, I stood up and started running again, to get as far away from the burnt-out aircraft as possible.

Suddenly I heard something behind me and looked around to see a small reconnaissance vehicle with three Afrika Korps soldiers closing rapidly on me, so I stopped running and turned to face them. One of them could speak some English and said, "For you, the war is over. Every day is now Sunday."

Coster would spend the rest of the war in successive Italian and German POW camps, including Stalag Luft III of 'Great Escape' fame, but that is another story.

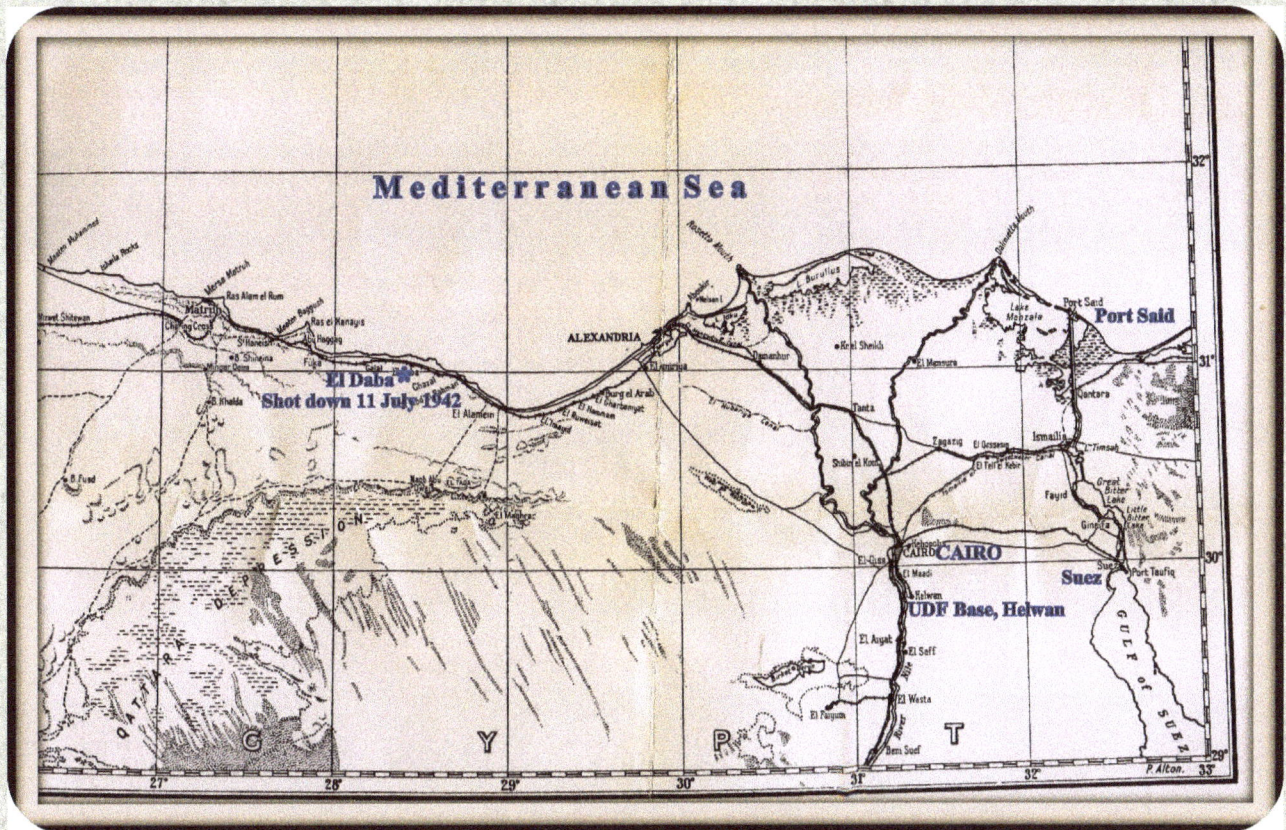

'Shot down over North Africa'.

Capt Keith Robert Coster at the end of World War Two.
(Photo Gerry van Tonder)

Temporary Sergeant Theodore Owen Nel BCR
1 (Independent) Company, The Rhodesia Regiment
Bronze Cross of Rhodesia (BCR)

Theo Nel's medal group. His BCR is second from the right.
The first five medals from the left are South African, earned after the Rhodesian bush war.

Citation:

On 28 August 1977 Sergeant Theodore Owen Nel was in command of a six man patrol following up a group of terrorists estimated to be between eight and twelve in number when the patrol came under heavy fire at close range. Sergeant Nel immediately engaged the enemy killing one of the sentries and forcing the terrorists to abandon their position. Sergeant Nel and the patrol pursued the terrorists for 25 minutes before locating a further recently vacated resting place where they found thirty four packs which had been abandoned by the terrorists. Whilst recovering the packs the patrol again came under heavy fire from the terrorist group now estimated to be over thirty. A fierce fire fight ensued with the terrorists intent on driving off the numerically smaller patrol. Sergeant Nel and his men refused to be driven from their position despite the fact that ammunition was running dangerously low. Because of this Sergeant Nel decided to utilize a terrorist rocket launcher which he had seen amongst the terrorist packs in the open river bed. With little regard for his own personal safety he made two forays under heavy automatic fire and recovered both the launcher and ammunition. Sergeant Nel then moved to a position where he engaged the main terrorist position with accurate fire. The terrorists broke contact and fled abandoning a large quantity of war materials, including eighteen landmines.

There is no doubt that Sergeant Nel's brave and calculated actions forced the terrorists from their positions and saved what could have been a dangerous situation for his patrol. This action typifies the courage, determination and skill that Sergeant Nel has consistently displayed throughout his service. His resolute pursuit of the enemy has resulted in him being involved in a large number of successful contacts in the past two years.

Bronze Cross of Rhodesia.
(Gerry van Tonder collection)

This unit became part of the Rhodesian African Rifles at the beginning of 1978, by which time Sergeant Nel had become the tracker platoon commander operating in support of 1 and 4 (Independent) Companies, Rhodesian African Rifles. His act of gallantry recognised by this award occurred when his unit was still part of the Rhodesia Regiment.

Fort Umlugulu Cemetery 1896

Herbert Plumer, a major with the York and Lancaster Regiment, had been given the local rank of Lieutenant Colonel and tasked by the British High Commissioner in South Africa, Sir Hercules Robinson, to raise a relief force to quell the amaNdebele uprising in Matabeleland in 1896.

The corps eventually numbered 850 active men, including some 400 from the Bechuanaland Border Police and the BSACo Police. The balance was mainly made up of miners, engineers, farmers and clerks. Most were English-born colonials, with a contingent of about 200 English and Dutch Afrikanders.

Elements of the task force were soon engaged in action with the rebel impis at Gwaai, Umguza, Khami, and the mission station at Hope Fountain where a fort had been erected. By July, all that remained was to neutralise the rebel strongholds in the Matopos, a major challenge given the extremely rough, boulder-strewn hills of the spiritual home of the amaNdebele. At the time, chief scout Robert Baden-Powell described the terrain as "...a tract of intricate broken country, containing a jumble of granite-boulder mountains and bush-grown gorges..."

Plumer set up a new camp on Mr Usher's farm, on the northern approaches to the Matopo Hills, with Fort Umlugulu to the east the expedition's main base. After weeks of skirmishing in the broken terrain, Cecil Rhodes met with amaNdebele chiefs—the Great Indaba—on 21 August, marking the end of the rebellion.

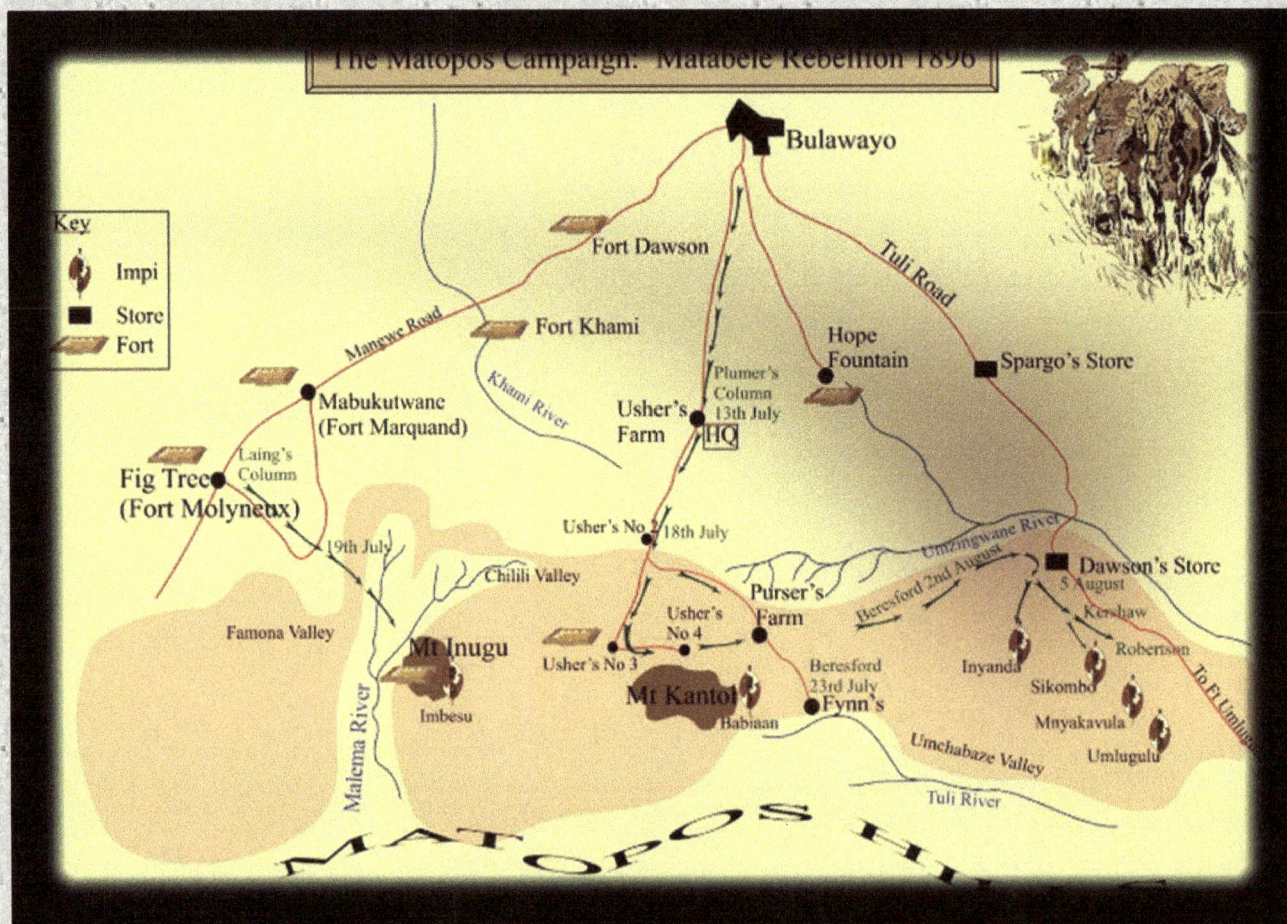

(Map Col Dudley Wall)

Documentation, including The London Gazette of 5 April 1898, contemporary accounts and memorials confirm that Fort Umlugulu is the final resting place of the following 13 men:

Trooper Peter BENNETT (MMP), KIA, Inugu, 20 July 1896
Trooper William Henry BUSH (MMP), KIA, Inugu, 20 July 1896
Corporal John HALL (BeFF), KIA, Inugu, 20 July 1896
Trooper William BERN (BFF), KIA, Inugu, 27 July 1896
Trooper Lawrence CHEVES (BFF), KIA, Inugu, 27 July 1896
Trooper Edward Runnell LITTLE (MRF), shooting accident, Spargo's, 3 August 1896
Battery Sergeant Major Alexander AINSLIE (MMP), KIA, Sikombo, 5 August 1896
Sergeant William GIBB (MRF), KIA, Sikombo, 5 August 1896
Lieutenant Hubert John Antony HERVEY (MRF), DoW 6 August 1896, sustained 5 August, Sikombo
Trooper Evelyn HOLMES (MRF), DoW 9 August 1896, sustained 5 August, Sikombo
Sergeant Archibald INNES-KERR (MRF), KIA, Sikombo, 5 August 1896
Major Frederick E. KERSHAW (MRF), KIA Sikombo, 5 August 1896
Sergeant Oswald Douglas MCCLOSKIE (MRF), KIA, Sikombo, 5 August 1896

(MRF: KIA: Killed in Action; DoW: Died of Wounds; Matabeleland Relief Force; MMP: Matabeleland Mounted Police; BFF: Bulawayo Field Force; BeFF: Belingwe Field Force)

The only grave that can be identified today is that of Lt Hervey,
prominent with its black stone cross and etched slab.
Metal crosses can be seen, and although it is known who is buried in the cemetery,
the name plates have all been stolen.
(Photo Alan Bryant)

Rhodesian

Despatches

Issue No. 3, March 2021

CONTENTS

It has been 125 years since the outbreak of the Matabele and Mashona rebellions of 1896, when the indigenous amaNdebele and Shona-speaking ethnic groups in Rhodesia rose up against the presence of white settlers, murdering hundreds of innocent men, women and children.

I have been commissioned to write a feature article on the Mashona Rebellion for the April 2021 issue of the *Britain at War* magazine, my first 'all-Rhodesian' feature for this premier British periodical. I will provide details in due course.

Defences at the laagered Fort Salisbury, 1896. (NAZ)

My prime research source is the British South Africa Company's official 1898 document, *Reports on the Native Disturbances in Rhodesia*, as it gives raw fact without the embellishment of either academic speculation or nationalist indictment. Something I did encounter, especially online, is the more recent 'labelling' of the events of the 1890s in that territory which became known as Rhodesia.

The armed and uniformed Pioneer Column established Fort Salisbury in September 1890, after having established, among others, a garrison at Fort Victoria. The next landmark event, and one that would permanently change the profile of the new territory, was in November 1893 when combined columns of troops from Salisbury and Victoria took guBulawayo, effectively bringing to an end the amaNdebele kingdom under their monarch Lobengula. This was the Matabele War, characterised by the battles of Bembesi and Shangani (not to be confused with Allan Wilson's patrol), and not the 'First' Matabele War.

Bulawayo laager 1896.(NAZ)

Blaming the settlers for the rinderpest, plagues of locusts and a drought, the amaNdebele rose up in March 1896. This is wrongly referred to as the Second Matabele War—it was the Matabele Rebellion. In June that year, some of the Shona-speaking chiefdoms also rose up. Amazingly, this seems to now be lost in the term 'Second Matabele War', when, in fact, it was the Mashona Rebellion. The two rebellions were noticeably different.

The martial amaNdebele, only three years after the demise of their king, rose up as one. In Mashonaland, there was no such unified uprising and no regimental military structure with which to persecute the rebellion. Strong minds such as chiefs Mashayamombe and Makoni fuelled revolt in their own areas. In Mashonaland, the mediums Nehanda and Kaguvi wielded far greater power, revered for their connection to the 'supreme being', Mwari, via ancestral spirits, or mhondoro. This unwavering spiritual belief would, among the Shona, play a significant role in the Rhodesian Bush War of the 1970s.

BSAP 1896.

Johan Colenbrander CB

To most of us the momentous Great Indaba in the Matopos on 22 August 1896 is well-remembered. It was taught at school and became an integral part of the folklore of Rhodesia from that date. In this the first of several meetings that would be conducted over five weeks with indunas of the amaNdebele rebels, four white men sat on an anthill, facing a group of amaNdebele, tired and hungry; defeat written on their faces. The drought, rinderpest and the bewildering might of the Maxim machine gun had forced them into their final refuge in the sacred hills of the Matopos.

Native Scout Jan Grootboom had, under a white flag, escorted the 40 indunas down from the hills, to where Cecil Rhodes waited to commence peace talks. With Rhodes were surgeon Dr Hans Sauer, a companion and member of the Jameson Raid; a Mr De Vere Stent, War Correspondent with the Cape Times; and Johan Colenbrander, the interpreter. Colenbrander was reluctant to put his life at risk, but a payment from Rhodes of 1,000 guineas ensured his presence. Mollie Colenbrander, Johan's wife and the only woman allowed in camp, handed out pistols to the men before they set out, with Sauer shoving one on each pocket, but Rhodes preferred to go unarmed.

Johan Colenbrander and his wife Mollie.

Johan Wilhelm Colenbrander was born in Pinetown, Natal, on 1 November 1856, the son of Dutch parents who had emigrated from Java to Natal in 1854. As a youth, he spent most of his time on the veld, becoming highly skilled in shooting and horsemanship, as well as becoming fluent in the language of the Zulu, people he shared his early adventures with.

At 15, he enlisted as a trumpeter in the Natal Mounted Rifles, and at 18, during the Anglo-Zulu campaign against Ceteswayo, he suffered a serious head wound from a Zulu battle axe, as well as several assegai wounds during a prolonged bout of close combat with a Zulu warrior.

After the war, Colenbrander briefly served in Zululand as secretary to the white 'chief', John Dunn, also becoming commander of his army. He then opened a trading store at Usibepu, but with in-house Zulu rivalry still prevalent in the area, he lost his business.

In 1883, Colenbrander married Maria 'Mollie' Mullins who, herself an excellent shottist and horsewoman and almost as proficient as her husband in the Zulu language, proved to be a perfect partner. The couple moved to Swaziland where Colenbrander set up a trading store, but in 1888 he was again to face financial ruin when his oxen died from the tsetse fly-borne sleeping sickness while on a trek to Delagoa Bay.

Moving to Johannesburg to take up a position as a claims inspector, Colenbrander met E.R. Renny-Tailyour, who asked Colenbrander to accompany him to guBulawayo in Matabeleland and the court of Lobengula, from whom he was hoping to obtain a concession. It was here that Lobengula developed a respectful relationship with this forceful but bright and cheerful white man who spoke isiNdebele like one of his own. It was therefore to this trusted friend that Lobengula relied on to interpret the concession proposals submitted by Rhodes' emissary, Charles Rudd, and indeed it was due to Colenbrander that the so-called Rudd Concession became a reality, paving the way for Rhodes to venture into this part of the hinterland.

To further satisfy Lobengula of his intentions, it was agreed that two of the king's indunas, Babyaan and Umshete should visit Queen Victoria, with Colenbrander to go with as interpreter and, as it turned out, protector from London's Victorian society which revelled in the exotic, treating the unfortunate 'natives' as museum exhibits.

Cecil Rhodes deemed the London PR exercise such a success, that in 1890 he appointed Colenbrander as a representative of the Royal Chartered British South Africa Company. Three years later, Colenbrander was given the title Native Commissioner, and so Intaf, officially the Ministry of Internal Affairs, was born.

During the taking of guBulawayo in 1893, and the subsequent pursuit of Lobengula, Colenbrander saw active service in the flying column led by Major Patrick Forbes. After the demise of Allan Wilson and his small band of intrepid but deserted troopers, Colenbrander was with Forbes and Raaff as the ragged remnants of the column staggered back into guBulawayo. The Colenbranders then set up a permanent home in the 'liberated' Bulawayo, consisting of a few large huts, from where they hosted Bulawayo society.

Feeling that his role as Chief Native Commissioner was confined to the mundane recruitment of labour and the collection and disposal of loot cattle, in 1895 Colenbrander resigned his post. His position, which had been dubbed 'Collar-and-brand-em', clashed with the empathy he had for the amaNdebele nation, a tribe he had lived with for many years. Colenbrander was, however, in a position where he could foresee rebellion, undertones of dissent very evident to his 'native' ears.

The Great Indaba, a sketch by Robert Baden-Powell.

On March 28, 1896, the amaNdebele nation, deprived of a king and devastated by locusts and rinderpest of Biblical proportions, rose against the vulnerable white settlers. It was during this time, as mentioned earlier, that Colenbrander led a band of mainly black irregulars. With the capitulation of the rebels, it is said that an old amaNdebele woman, in response to overtures of peace, was sent to Fort Umlugulu in the Matopos to enquire of the officer commanding at the post if 'Johwane' was with the white people who wish to parley. The reference was to Colenbrander, who the amaNdebele still trusted with his fluency in their tongue to interpret the right words. The indunas would only come down from the Matopos hills if 'Johwane' was there.

Those present at the second indaba were in awe of Colenbrander's eloquent use of their native tongue, with the usual indigenous phraseology and flowery use of idiom or quip. This was Colenbrander's finest hour. He diffused a still belligerent atmosphere, causing the now convinced amaNdebele indunas to refer to him as umhlala n'yati—the tickbird (white egret) that removes irritations from the skin of a buffalo. In a dramatic reversal of his views on women, Rhodes was persuaded to allow Mollie Colenbrander to attend the second indaba, but she remained seated on her horse a short distance away, ready to race back to Fort Usher should events turn bad.

Subsequent to this, and before the third indaba, the Colenbranders moved their camp deeper into the Matopos, thereby allowing the amaNdebele easier access to discuss matters they were not yet certain of. It was during this uneasy interlude, typified by the apparent African disdain for time, that Rhodes had asked one of the indunas if they had any chance of succeeding against the settlers, the grizzled old man responded by admitting that yes, they had really felt they could rout the white man, but they now knew they could no more beat the white man than lick their own elbows. After the chief had left, both Colenbrander and Rhodes tried to lick their elbows – with no success.

Colonel J.W. Colenbrander.

Mollie Colenbrander, unable to have children, died of heart failure on October 9, 1900, aged 36. To get over his difficulties during this time, Colenbrander, now with the rank of Lieutenant Colonel, raised a mounted corps in South Africa called Kitchener's Fighting Scouts, to fight in the Anglo-Boer War. Operating in the west, in early 1901 Colenbrander led 830 troops deep into the Graaff Reinet area of the Cape Colony as British forces pursued the elusive Commandant Scheepers. In April that year, Colenbrander was back in the theatre to the north and east of Pietersburg in the northern Transvaal, enjoying successes against the van Rensburg and Venter Commandos.

By the end of the year, Colenbrander had been deployed to the west, as combined British forces tried to corner General Koos de la Rey. For the first half of 1902, Colenbrander and his unit were engaged in chasing down Commandant Beyers. Now dubbed by Transvaal Republicans the scourge of the Northern Transvaal, the tenacious Colenbrander hounded his enemy in the vast expanses of the Highveld from Pietersburg to Warm Baths. By May 1902, Colenbrander had secured substantial tracts of territory, the defeated Republicans reeling under the systematic persistent onslaught of the British forces.

Colenbrander was twice mentioned in despatches. The first on March 12 1897, for his contribution to the quashing of rebellions in Rhodesia, and the second on April 8, 1902, as the commanding officer of Kitchener's Fighting Scouts during the Anglo-Boer War.

On June 27, 1902, Colenbrander was appointed a Member of the Military Division of the Third Class of the Most Honourable Order of the Bath.

Colenbrander's marriage to his second wife, Yvonne Nunn, was short lived, as she died in 1905, only three years after they were married. The 59 year-old Colenbrander later offered his services at the outbreak of the Great War but, understandably, the British War Office turned down the 58-year-old's offer. He then settled in Johannesburg, where he was to become technical adviser as well as actor in an I.W. Schlesinger film production of the Anglo-Zulu War of 1879.

During a scene shot at the Klip River near Johannesburg, Colenbrander, playing the role of Lord Chelmsford en route to saving the beleaguered garrison at Rorke's Drift, fell as his horse caught its legs in some wire as they were crossing the river. Freeing himself from his mount, undaunted Colenbrander started to swim to the bank of the river, only to be trampled to death in the mud by the cavalry of horses that he had been leading. It was Sunday, February 10, 1918. Colenbrander was 61 years old.

A tragic end to the man described as a soldier, businessman, interpreter, agent and hunter, and father of Internal Affairs (Intaf). Colenbrander is buried in the Brixton Cemetery in Johannesburg.

Badge of the
Companion of the Order of the Bath, Military Division.

Rhodesian Bush War , Masoso, 19 July 1975

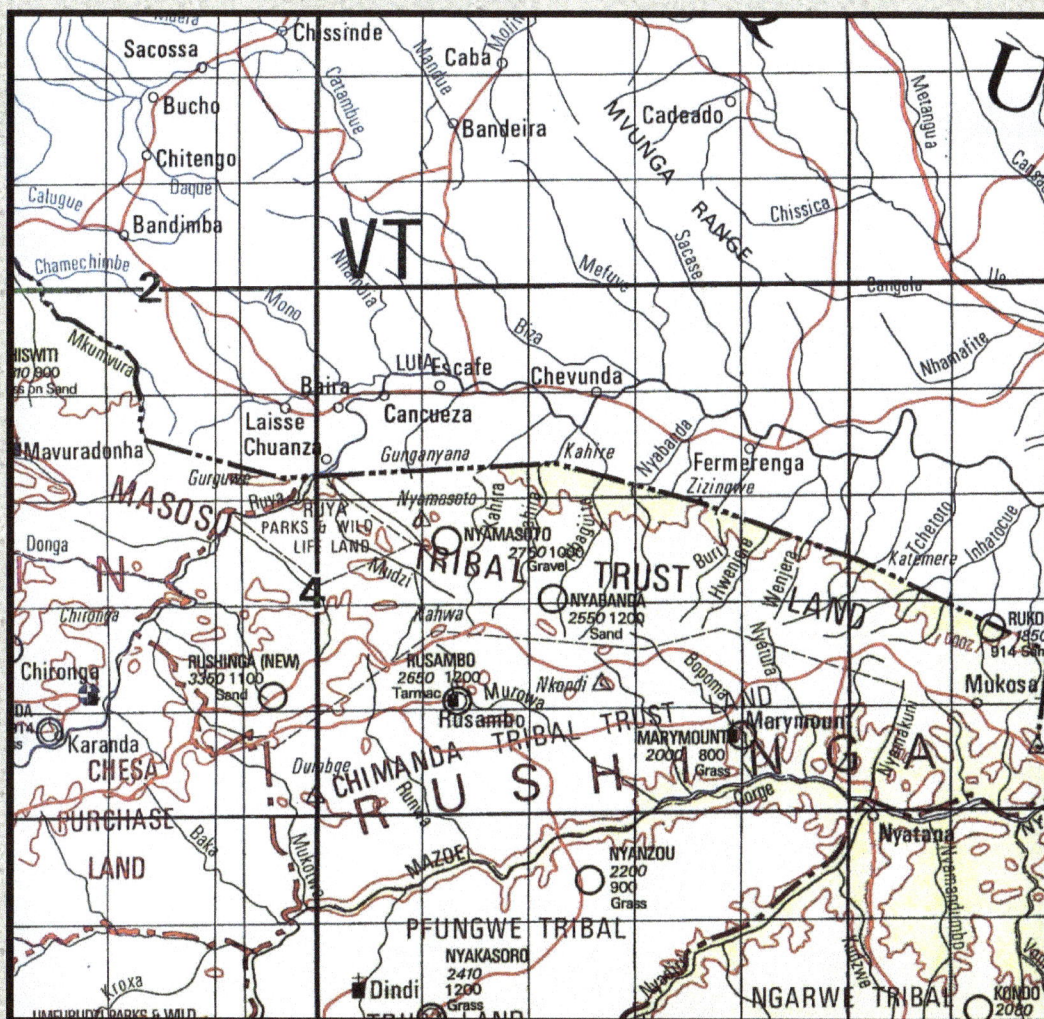

Masoso Tribal Trust Land, Rushinga district. The circles on the map indicate airstrips.

Being mid-winter in Central Africa, the seasonal rivers and streams throughout much of Rhodesia were dry, sandy and, in many cases, strewn with large boulders. The river banks, however, carry evidence of earlier flooding, deeply eroded in places with tree roots marking the entrances to cave-like cavities in the steep sides of a water course. In the country's northern border with a belligerent Mozambique and haven to ZANLA guerrillas, the Masoso Tribal Trust Land (TTL) straddles the Rushinga and Mt Darwin districts, east of the Mvuradonha Mountains. It was in this remote wilderness that Rhodesian security Forces conducted seek-and-destroy patrols, with enemy sightings backed up by Fire Force support from a nearby Forward Air Field, in this case Mt Darwin.

On 19 July 1975, two trackers, Rifleman Hennie Potgieter of 2 Commando, the Rhodesian Light Infantry (RLI), and Warrant Officer II Taz Bain of the 2nd Battalion, the Rhodesia Regiment (2RR), went ahead of a 2 Commando patrol along a dry riverbed, but progress was tortuous around and over boulders and rocks. Thick bush lined the sides of the riverbed. Unbeknown to them, a gang of ZANLA guerrillas were secreted in a cave in the side of the river bank, about a metre above the river bed itself, an ideal position for an ambush. As the unsuspecting soldiers came within ten metres of the guerrilla hideout, the guerrilla opened fire, seriously wounding both men with multiple gunshots.

Great uncertainty ensued, as their fellow RLI soldiers on the riverbank struggled to see either the two wounded men or where the guerrillas were firing from. A K-Car (helicopter gunship) was also unsuccessful in flushing the terrorists out.

At this stage, Corporal John Coey, a medic on attachment to the RLI from the Rhodesian Army Medical Corps, reacted to moans coming from the wounded men by jumping into the riverbed. Unfortunately, Coey was not to know that the guerrilla position was right there, and as he landed on the soft sand, he was fired upon, sustaining a head wound.

Further sticks from the RLI 7 and 10 troops were deployed as stop groups, while Lieutenant Joe du Plooy, also of 2 Commando, started lobbing grenades into the riverbed to try and get the guerrillas to reveal their position. Again failing to solicit any response from below, du Plooy then made the decision to skirmish along the riverbed to where his wounded men lay.

L-R: Sgt. Ed Fouche, 2 Lt. Joe du Plooy, Lt. Gideon Kriel and Maj. Charlie Aust (OC) 2 Commando, Rhodesian Light Infantry, July 1974.

As they made their way around some boulders, the Rhodesians again drew fire from the concealed guerrillas. Lance Corporal Jannie de Beer fell, a fatal gunshot wound to an iliac artery, while du Plooy sustained a graze to his head, and a third trooper was wounded. Casualties were mounting, but the position of the guerrillas or the condition of the three shot men remained unknown. Du Plooy, against his wishes, was ordered to be casevaced back to base, and Corporal Ronald 'Butch' Alexander assumed control of the situation on the ground.

Through that afternoon, sporadic fire between the Rhodesian soldiers and the ZANLA cadres dwindled, until eventually the enemy stopped firing completely. As the light began to fade, there was still no resolution to the situation, and the three stricken men lay unattended on the riverbed.

In Mt Darwin, Lieutenant Bob MacKenzie of the Special Air Service (SAS) had been monitoring the situation to the northeast and, upon realising that the day was ending with the condition of three members of the security forces remaining uncertain, made the decision to immediately respond by helicopter. Rounding up fellow SAS volunteers in Mt Darwin, MacKenzie also found that two helicopter pilots of No. 7 Squadron, the Rhodesian Air Force, were more than willing to transport his men to the Masoso, fully understanding the hazards flying Alouette III helicopters at night posed.

With no night-flying equipment, a moon that night assisted the pilots with keeping the horizon visible. An hour later, the SAS men were at the scene, where they were met by an anxious Corporal Alexander. He confirmed in a quick briefing that the riverbed area was silent, and that the position of their fallen brothers-in-arms was still to be pinpointed, therefore not knowing if they were still alive. It was not known either if the guerrillas had moved on as they had not fired their weapons for some time.

The ubiquitous Alouette III helicopter, mainstay of the Rhodesian bush war about to emplane fire-force troops.,

With two members of the SAS contingent providing cover with night sights fitted to their rifles, MacKenzie and Alexander crawled to the edge of the riverbank, and in the moonlight finally managed to see the three wounded men lying close to each other on the riverbed. There was no movement from any of them. There was, however, no way of knowing if the guerrillas were still in their hideout, so MacKenzie got the RLI troops to lob grenades, including white phosphorus, into the riverbed. This was followed by an extended period of firing into possible guerrillas positions, but there was no return fire.

Undaunted, and wishing to end the on-going uncertainty about the fate of the Rhodesian soldiers and the whereabouts of the guerrilla stronghold, MacKenzie felt that the only remaining option was to go down into the riverbed. Taking one of his men, armed with an MAG, and Alexander, the latter insisting he go along to see to his fellow troops, MacKenzie stripped off his webbing and, leaving his rifle behind and armed only with a pistol and a grenade, entered the riverbed 150 metres downstream from the possible guerrilla position

With nerves at breakpoint, the trio inched their way along, the moonlight providing guiding visibility, but at the same time creating shadows and questionable shapes. Then suddenly, the palpable tension was broken, as the extremely loud clatter of bursts of fire from the MAG shattered the stillness. The MAG-gunner, feeling uncomfortable about something ahead, fired over the heads of MacKenzie and Alexander, sending intermittent red tracer streaking towards the riverbank. Abrupt silence followed. Still no response from the guerrillas.

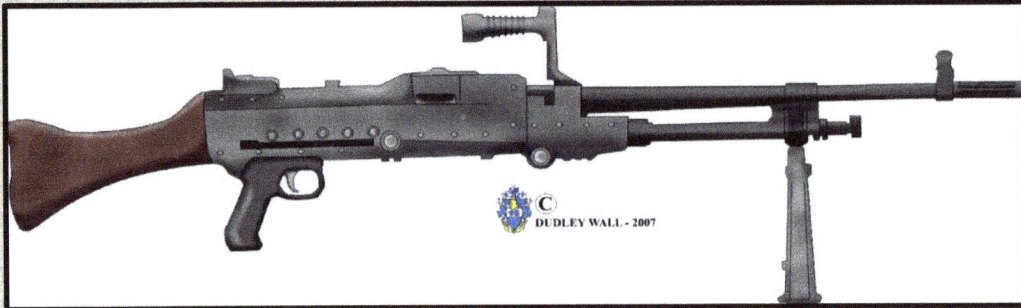

Belgian FN MAG (*Mitrailleuse d'Appui Général*) 7.62 mm general-purpose machine gun.
(Col Dudley Wall)

Eventually, the men reached their fallen comrades, their worst fears realised as they failed to find any traces of life. MacKenzie was also able, at last, to identify the cave where the terrorists had been firing from, his eyes drawn to globules of white phosphorus burning on the walls of the cave. After lobbing further grenades into the cave, MacKenzie crept into the cave, only to find that the guerrillas had made good their escape. The guerrillas has escaped across a maize field and in between stop groups, taking with them the MAG and ammunition carried by one of the Rhodesian soldiers.

Tracking was made difficult for the SAS trackers the following morning, the guerrillas' tracks blending in with those of locals in the area. The MAG, however, was found, the heavy weapon abandoned by the fleeing terrorists. This marked the end of a tragic and frustrating engagement with guerrillas, one which was typical of the nature of Rhodesia's bush war, the enemy taking full advantage of difficult and often treacherous terrain. Four lost their lives, but in all of this, the Rhodesian soldiers refused to give up on their brothers, unselfishly placing their own lives at great risk.

725702 Cpl John Coey's final resting place in the Ohio Hills, USA.

Corporal John Alan Coey (24), one of several Americans to serve in the Rhodesian Army, enlisted in the SAS on March 26, 1972, seeing his first action in Mozambique's Tete province. In 1974, he became an instructor in the RLI; later part of Support Commando, specialising in tracking, mortars and armoured vehicles. Eventually he became a medic, trained at Llewellin Barracks, in Bulawayo. He participated in 65 fire-force missions, helping to pioneer the combat medic concept with the RLI. John, initially buried in Que Que, was exhumed when it became evident that Rhodesia's days were numbered, and he is now buried in the Ohio hills where a small American flag adorns his grave. He believed his destiny was in Rhodesia, the last bastion against Communism.

Cpl John Coey in Rhodesian SAS uniform.

Captain Johannes Matheus 'Joe' du Plooy (26) was killed on 6 September 1979 when the SADF Puma helicopter in which he was being transported to Mapai, Mozambique on Op Uric, was shot down by an RPG-7 rocket. The aircraft, with the call-sign Hotel 4, was hit behind the pilot's seat, causing it to crash and burst into flames. Nine of the dead were RLI.

Corporal 'Butch' Alexander was killed in action on 16 December 1976, during a combined RLI/SAS attack on a ZANLA camp at Rambanayi, Mozambique. The camp, also housing a platoon of Tanzanian troops, was defended by a complex of trenches and bunkers covered by large logs and soil, and it was when Butch jumped into the command bunker occupied by the enemy, that he was shot and killed.

Lieutenant Gerald Keogh MC (**WWII**)

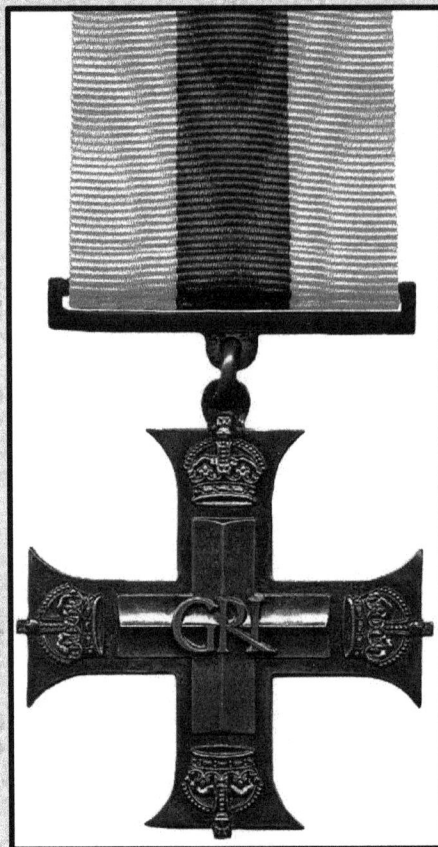

Military Cross (George VI).

26 September 1940:
Lieutenant Gerald KEOGH,
The Rhodesia Regiment
Attached the Somaliland Camel Corps.
Recommendation citation as contained in War Office Document 373/28 of August 19, 1940.
General Archibald Wavell, Commander-in-Chief, Middle East, recommended the award of Military Cross:

> I wish to bring to notice the conspicuous service rendered by Lieutenant Gerald Keogh, Rhodesia Regiment, attached Somaliland Camel Corps, full details of which have, owing to the isolated position of his company, only just been received.
>
> On the 24th June 1940, BURAMO station was occupied by an Italian Force which included regular troops A.F.Vs and machine-guns.
>
> On 26th June Lieutenant KEOGH was despatched with one camel troop with orders to obtain information regarding the situation at BURAMO and if the circumstances were favourable to carry out a destructive raid.
>
> On 27th June the troop arrived in the vicinity of BURAMO and was joined by 40 Illalos [Somali tribesmen]. For two days the troop remained in concealment and sent back valuable information. On the night 29/30th June a raid on the station was carried out.

The approach of the party was detected by the defenders and heavy fire was opened. Nevertheless the attack was pressed until the buildings occupied by the Europeans were reached. These buildings were attacked with grenades, resulting as has subsequently been ascertained in the death of two and possibly three Europeans. Withdrawal was then carried out in an orderly manner.

Lieutenant KEOGH has subsequently carried out another successful night raid against an Italian post at DUMUK.

I consider that in organising and leading these raids Lieutenant KEOGH has shown marked courage, resource and determination deserving of special recognition. I recommend him for the award of the MILITARY CROSS.

(Charlie Johnson Payne, 'Snaffles')

Menin Gate

In the summer of 2014, my wife and I went on a guided coach tour of the Western Front battlefields of World War One. At the time, I was assisting Hugh Bomford with the Rhodesia Regiment book project, so I went on then trip with a list of names of members of the regiment who, having completed their active service in the German South West Africa and German East Africa theatres of war, had volunteered for wartime service in Europe. A large number had enlisted with 1 South Africa Infantry (1SAI).

At the imposing Menin Gate Memorial, in Ieper, Belgium, the lives of 55,000 British and Commonwealth troops who fell in battle on the Ypres Salient, and whose graves are not known, are commemorated.

Opened by Field Marshal Lord Herbert Plumer in 1927, the Menin Gate Memorial arches one of the main thoroughfares into the town of Ieper.

Whilst the memorial carries the names of 21 members of the Rhodesia Regiment, unfortunately I only had sufficient time to find and photograph those 10 men who had served and fallen with the 1 South African Infantry:

```
ABBOTT J.H.      GOWING H. J.        HUBIE  S. R
ACKERMANN A.J. GRIESSEL A. J. J.  HUTTON R.
     KELLEHER  J. J.   WOOD  W. F.
     KING  N. A.        WRIGHT  R. M. S.
```

Other Books by the Author

Berlin Blockade: Soviet Chokehold and the Great Allied Airlift 1948–1949
Chesterfield's Military Heritage
Derby in 50 Buildings
Echoes of the Coventry Blitz
Inchon Landing: MacArthur's Korean War Masterstroke September 1950
Irgun: Revisionist Zionism 1931–1948
Korean War, Allied Surge: Pyongyang Falls, UN Sweep to the Yalu October 1950
Lieutenant-General Keith Coster: A Life in Uniform
Malayan Emergency: Triumph of the Running Dogs 1948–1960
Mansfield Through Time
North Korea Invades the South: Across the 38th Parallel, June 1950
North Korean Onslaught: UN Stand at the Pusan Perimeter August-September 1950
Korean War, Chinese Invasion: People's Liberation Army Crosses the Yalu October 1950-March
   1951
Korean War, Imjin River: Fall of the Glosters to the Armistice April 1951-July 1953
North of the Red Line: Recollections of the Border War by Members of the South African Armed
   Forces: 1966–1989
Nottingham's Military Legacy
Operation Lighthouse: Intaf in the Rhodesian Bush War 1972–1980
Red China: Mao Crushes Chiang's Kuomintang, 1949
Rhodesia Regiment 1899–1981
Rhodesian African Rifles/Rhodesia Native Regiment Book of Remembrance
Rhodesian Combined Forces Roll of Honour 1966-1981
Sheffield's Military Legacy
Sino-Indian War: October–November 1962
SS Einsatzgruppen: Nazi Death Squads 1939–1945
South African Air Force: The Flying Springboks 1939-80
Under the Muchakata Tree, Jim Latham (comp & ed.)

Feature Article Writing

Britain at War magazine (UK)
Classic Military Vehicle magazine (UK)
Royal Artillery Journal (UK)
Nongqai publications (South Africa, online)
Rhodesian Services Association